To Susan Schulman

Library of Congress Cataloging-in-Publication Data

Harness, Cheryl.
Flags over America : a star-spangled story / Cheryl Harness.
pages cm
1. Flags—United States—Juvenile literature. 2. Flags—United States—History—Juvenile literature.
I. Title.
CR113.H317 2014
929.9'20973—dc23
2014000629

Text and illustrations copyright © 2014 Cheryl Harness
Published in 2014 by Albert Whitman & Company
ISBN 978-0-8075-2470-1
Printed in China.
10 9 8 7 6 5 4 3 2 1 BP 18 17 16 15 14

The design is by Cheryl Harness and Nick Tiemersma.

For more information about Albert Whitman & Company,
visit our web site at www.albertwhitman.com.

Some say Americans carried this Continental Flag at the Battle of Bunker Hill.

"Each time I look at that flag, I am reminded that our destiny is stitched together like those fifty stars and thirteen stripes."–President Barack Obama

Introduction

For the many ceremonies planned in 1892 for the 400th anniversary of Christopher Columbus's voyage to America, Francis Bellamy, a minister, wrote a patriotic pledge that students might recite:

> *"I pledge allegiance to my Flag and the Republic for which it stands, one nation, indivisible, with liberty and justice for all."*

In 1954, Congress revised Bellamy's words. So it is that countless Americans put their right hands over their hearts and say:

> *"I pledge allegiance to the flag of the United States of America, and to the republic for which it stands, one nation under God, indivisible, with liberty and justice for all."*

Just thirty-one simple words about a flag, something that is not simple at all. Whether it's flapping from a pole, fluttering from a balcony, or stitched onto a cap, a flag is a story.

A ship on the horizon!

An army on the march!

People shade their eyes. They squint into the sun or the smoke of battle. They look for a far-off flash of color, a sign that will say: Is it a friend? Or an enemy on the way?

Phoenician merchant ship,
750 BCE

Since ancient times, people made designs that stood for themselves, their lands, their leaders, or their faiths.

Symbol for the Egyptian god Horus, 3,400 BCE

They put them on their soldiers' shields or on the sails of their ships. They fastened their stitched and painted symbols, or *standards*, onto sticks and raised high their flags, their *colors*, to be seen from afar.

Roman legion soldier and flag, 45 BCE

Viking raven flag, 1000 AD

With their flags, people showed who they were—and, in time of war, what they were fighting for. When an army had lost too much, waving a white flag became the custom, meaning, "let's talk this over" or we *surrender*, "we give up."

Flag for Kublai Khan's fleet, Mongolia, late 1200s AD

French battle standard, 1300 AD

Banner for Richard I of England, 1189 AD

Jolly Roger pirate flag, early 1700s AD

NORTH AMERICA 1763

SPANISH LANDS

BRITISH Territory

FRENCH LANDS for now

HUDSON BAY

BAFFIN ISLAND

LABRADOR SEA

NEWFOUND LAND

claimed by NY & NH

MAINE, part of MASS.

NEW YORK

NH

MASS.

Boston

PENN.

CT

R.I.

New York City

NJ

Philadelphia

DEL.

MD.

VIRGINIA

NORTH CAROLINA

SOUTH CAROLINA

GEORGIA

FLORIDA

GULF of MEXICO

New Orleans

BAHAMAS

CUBA

JAMAICA

HISPANIOLA

PUERTO RICO

TROPIC of CANCER

CARIBBEAN SEA

Over hundreds of years, small ships flying the flags of their nations sailed far across the world's oceans. Kings and queens sent explorers to Asia, Africa, and to the Americas to gather valuable spices, slaves, gold, and furs and to spread their religious beliefs. By the 1500s, the flag of Spain flew over settlements in the Western Hemisphere. In the 1700s, France's flag fluttered over forts in North American forests and along the Mississippi River.

And where the Atlantic Ocean met the North American coast, the flag of Great Britain flew over thirteen colonies. But in 1763, trouble began between Britain's King George III and his distant American subjects.

After long years of war, Great Britain had won most of France's North American land. The colonists and Native Americans fought so much over the land that British troops had to keep the peace, a costly business. To pay for it, British lawmakers started taxing the colonists, but they did it in such a stern, heavy-handed way that the relationship between the Americans and the British turned sour and angry.

The colonists began gathering around *liberty poles* with flags that stood for what they wanted: to be represented in Great Britain's legislature, just as if they lived in England. When the king's lawmakers put a tax on tea, the colonists stopped buying it because they'd had no say in that tax law. That was not fair!

After angry Bostonians dumped boxes of tea into the sea, King George III closed their harbor in 1774, putting Boston merchants out of business! The irate colonists chose men to form a Continental Congress.

LIBERTY

The king, upset with this show of unity, sent more red-coated troops. On April 19, 1775, fighting broke out between these *redcoats* and the colonists in Lexington and Concord. The Revolutionary War had begun! The Continental Congress chose George Washington, a veteran soldier from Virginia, to lead an army of patriots to fight the fight of their lives.

STAMP ACT FLAG

Boston's Sons of Liberty used this flag in their protests against Great Britain's 1765 Stamp Act. A tax stamp had to be put on legal papers, newspapers—even playing cards!

PINE TREE FLAG

The pine tree symbol in this flag (1775) and the New England Flag (1707–1775) came from the Penacooks (Algonquin for "Children of the Pine Tree"), Native Americans of eastern New England.

TAUNTON FLAG

In October 1774, patriots in Taunton, Massachusetts, raised this flag. Great Britain's symbol in the upper left corner showed their loyalty, but they wanted liberty too, to be treated like fully free British citizens.

NEW ENGLAND FLAG

From 1707 until 1775, when the Revolutionary War began, this flag was popular with New Englanders.

BEDFORD·FLAG

The motto on this flag, *Vince Aut Morire*, means "Conquer or Die." Some say that Bedford, Massachusetts, soldiers carried this flag in the battle of Concord, April 19, 1775.

FLAG OF THE GREEN MOUNTAIN BOYS

In May 1775, the Green Mountain Boys, soldiers from Vermont, captured mighty Fort Ticonderoga in northern New York—along with the redcoats' cannons. The Americans needed them! Bostonian Henry Knox and teams of men and oxen hauled the big guns 300 miles over rough, icy country so George Washington could use them to force the British out of Boston on March 17, 1776.

Revolutionary America bristled with flags.

EASTON FLAG

When the Declaration of Independence was read out to the citizens of Easton, Pennsylvania, on July 8, 1776, the townspeople hoisted this version of the stars and stripes.

FORT MOULTRIE FLAG

Colonel William Moultrie designed this flag, also known as the *Liberty Flag*, in 1775. It flew over the Americans' little fort near Charleston, South Carolina. The British shot the flag away, but the colonists stopped them from capturing their important harbor town on June 28, 1776.

GADSDEN FLAG

Colonel Christopher Gadsden presented this flag to the Continental Congress in 1775 as a standard for the new Continental Navy. From those first patriot sailors grew the United States Marines.

GRAND UNION FLAG

On New Year's Day 1776, George Washington ordered this flag, also known as the *Continental Colors*, flown at Somerville, Massachusetts. The stripes stood for the thirteen colonies, but Great Britain's colors were there too, in the flag's upper left corner, its *canton*.

At the Continental Congress in Philadelphia, such men as Benjamin Franklin, John Adams, and Thomas Jefferson argued over the crisis. Little by little, their talk turned to a shocking, dangerous idea: though it would mean war, the colonies should break away from Britain and form their own nation!

On steamy July 4, 1776, the delegates agreed upon their bold Declaration of Independence. Meanwhile, a huge fleet of warships had come sailing into New York Harbor, all flying the flags of Great Britain. The king was determined to crush the Americans' rebellion.

As soon as fast riders could carry copies of the declaration, people gathered in America's towns to hear it read aloud. In New York City, General George Washington had the stirring words read to citizens and soldiers.

Afterward, the crowd toppled a huge metal statue of George III and melted it down into bullets. These rebellious Americans were going to need all they could get.

That summer and fall, the patriots fought and retreated from the British again and again.

By Christmas Eve, George Washington's cold, poorly equipped soldiers had come to the Pennsylvania side of the icy Delaware River. After many losses, their situation looked nearly hopeless. But the steadfast general led them across the dangerous river and on a long, freezing march to Trenton, New Jersey — where his troops won a remarkable victory and another at Princeton on January 3, 1777. Against all odds, the Americans were still in the fight.

With no idea if their young nation would even survive, the Continental Congress met for a bit of optimistic business on June 14, 1777.

Resolved, that the Flag of the thirteen United States shall be thirteen Stripes, alternate red and white; that the Union be thirteen Stars, white on a blue field, representing a new Constellation.

Francis Hopkinson, a delegate from New Jersey, may have designed the flag of the United States of America. He said that he did in a 1780 letter to the U.S. Congress. But there is no other proof, so a small cloud of history-mystery surrounds his claim.

So it is with the story of Betsy Ross, a Philadelphia seamstress and flag maker. According to her descendants, she told her family that she sewed her country's first flag, but we cannot definitely know.

After six years of war, the Continental Army was fighting at Yorktown, Virginia, when a British officer waved the white flag of surrender on October 19, 1781. The final peace treaty was signed in Paris on September 3, 1783, and the last British ships sailed from America on November 25, 1783.

Thin, tired George Washington led the victorious army into New York City past joyful citizens. The British had greased the flagpole, so a young soldier had to pound nails into it before he could pull down the British flag. Then he raised the starred-and-striped symbol of the newly independent United States of America.

$\mathcal{T}$he Americans were free of the hated British—weren't they?
Not entirely.

Before long, the Americans were caught in yet another big fight between Great Britain and France. Those two old lions were raiding U.S. vessels at sea, sparking violence on the Western frontier, and doing their best to sink their claws into the infant nation with all of its rich natural resources. In the War of 1812, the tiny United States was determined to prove itself as a nation among nations.

By August 1814, President and First Lady James and Dolley Madison and crowds of citizens were fleeing Washington DC. The British had set the White House and the U.S. Capitol on fire!

Now they were bearing down on Fort McHenry, where U.S. troops prepared to defend the key port city of Baltimore, Maryland. There, the defiant commander had ordered a huge U.S. flag, "so large that the British will have no trouble seeing it."

Baltimore seamstress Mary Pickersgill, her daughter, two nieces, and an African American servant girl had turned 400 yards of woolen cloth into a banner thirty feet wide and forty-two feet long!

Each of the banner's fifteen stripes was two feet wide. Each of its fifteen stars—thirteen for the original colonies plus two more for Vermont and Kentucky, which became states in 1791 and 1792—measured two feet from point to point!

A young lawyer, Francis Scott Key, was on a ship nearby on the thundering night of September 13, 1814, when the redcoats rained rockets and bombs onto Fort McHenry. He peered through the smoky dawn. Had the Americans held off the British? The sight of Mary Pickersgill's immense flag told him the answer.

Francis Scott Key poured out his relief and patriotic pride into a poem. He imagined the words sung to an old English tune, "To Anacreon in Heaven." Key's poem came to be called "The Star-Spangled Banner." Americans would sing it again and again, but hardly ever all of the verses.

Defense of Fort McHenry
Francis Scott Key (1779–1843)

1777

O say can you see, by the dawn's early light,
What so proudly we hail'd at the twilight's last gleaming,
Whose broad stripes and bright stars through the perilous fight
O'er the ramparts we watch'd were so gallantly streaming?
And the rocket's red glare, the bombs bursting in air,
Gave proof through the night that our flag was still there,
O say does that star-spangled banner yet wave
O'er the land of the free and the home of the brave?

On the shore dimly seen through the mists of the deep
Where the foe's haughty host in dread silence reposes,
What is that which the breeze, o'er the towering steep,
As it fitfully blows, half conceals, half discloses?
Now it catches the gleam of the morning's first beam,
In full glory reflected, now shines in the stream,
'Tis the star-spangled banner — O long may it wave
O'er the land of the free and the home of the brave!

1781

1795

And where is that band who so vauntingly swore,
That the havoc of war and the battle's confusion
A home and a Country should leave us no more?
Their blood has wash'd out their foul footstep's pollution.
No refuge could save the hireling and slave
From the terror of flight or the gloom of the grave,
And the star-spangled banner in triumph doth wave
O'er the land of the free and the home of the brave.

O thus be it ever when freemen shall stand
Between their lov'd homes and the war's desolation!
Blest with vict'ry and peace, may the heav'n rescued land
Praise the power that hath made and preserv'd us a nation!
Then conquer we must, when our cause it is just,
And this be our motto — "In God is our trust,"
And the star-spangled banner in triumph shall wave
O'er the land of the free and the home of the brave.

1960

Diplomats in Europe settled the War of 1812 before Christmas 1814. Neither side really won. But when U.S. troops who hadn't heard about the peace treaty defeated the British at New Orleans on January 8, 1815, Americans felt victorious indeed.

In time, in peace and in war, the British, French, and Americans became allies. And, in 1931, the United States chose for its anthem Francis Scott Key's song about a banner — and so much more. As much as the red stands for courage, the white for pure intention, and the blue for justice, our flag's stripes and stars stand for the bold colonies that we were and the fifty states, united in one nation, we have become. It's how we tell the world who we have been. And who we Americans are.

American Flag Timeline

June 14, 1777
The Continental Congress adopts a design for the U.S. flag.

September 14, 1814
Francis Scott Key writes a poem upon sighting "the star-spangled banner" still flying over Fort McHenry.

September 8, 1892
Francis Bellamy's Pledge of Allegiance is first published.

April 6, 1909
Robert Peary plants the American flag at the North Pole.

March 3, 1931
President Herbert Hoover signs the legislation to make "The Star-Spangled Banner" the national anthem of the United States.

June 22, 1942
President Franklin D. Roosevelt approves the Federal Flag Code with guidelines for displaying and respecting the U.S. flag.

August 3, 1949
President Harry S. Truman signs the bill calling for an official Flag Day every June 14.

July 4, 1960
President Dwight D. Eisenhower signs an executive order: with Hawaii's statehood, the twenty-seventh flag of the United States will have fifty stars, and it still does today.

May 22, 1963
National Geographic photographer Barry Bishop plants an American flag on the summit of Mount Everest.

July 5, 1968
U.S. Congress approves the first federal law against knowingly mutilating, trampling upon, defacing, or burning the American flag.

July 20, 1969
Astronaut Neil Armstrong plants the U.S. flag on the moon.

September 11, 2001
A flag flown at the World Trade Center survives attack and becomes a powerful symbol of national solidarity and courage.

Flag Glossary

badge   a person's or institution's emblem or design

banner   the flag of a nation, state, or army. A banner might be suspended behind a speaker's platform or carried at the head of a marching band.

bunting   a string of flags or the lightweight cloth used to make them

burgee   a ship's identifying flag, either swallowtailed or triangular

canton   the upper quarter of a flag closest to the flagpole

colors   the flags carried by military units or officers

ensign   a national flag flown on a ship

field   a flag's basic color or background

finial   a decorative ornament at the top of a staff

fly   the flapping end of a flag, farthest from the staff

guidon   the small flag carried by the leader of a military unit

halyard   the rope used to hoist—or raise—or lower a flag

heading or sleeve   the cloth tube for the rope at a flag's hoist—or the side by the pole

jack   the small flag at the bow of a ship

Jolly Roger   the traditional name for a pirate's skull-and-crossbones flag

motto   a phrase or saying representative of a flag's person, country, or organization

obverse   the front of a flag. The reverse is the back.

saltire   a flag with a diagonal cross

schwenkel   an extended streamer at the top of some flags

semaphore   a signaling system using a flag in each hand held in different positions for each letter of the alphabet. Using flags to communicate at sea goes back thousands of years.

standard   an important flag or vexilloid—a flag-like object. Today the term refers to the flag of a significant person such as a monarch.

swallowtail   a flag with a triangle cut out so its fly end is forked

vexillology   the study of flags